A Citizen's Guide to

The Economy

Heinemann
LIBRARY

Jenny Wales

H www.heinemann.co.uk/library
visit our website to find out more information about **Heinemann Library** books.

To order:
☎ Phone 44 (0) 1865 888066

▤ Send a fax to 44 (0) 1865 314091

▭ Visit the Heinemann Bookshop at www.heinemann.co.uk/library to browse our catalogue and order online.

First published in Great Britain by Heinemann Library, Halley Court, Jordan Hill, Oxford OX2 8EJ,
a division of Reed Educational and Professional Publishing Ltd.

Heinemann is a registered trademark of Reed Educational & Professional Publishing Limited.

OXFORD MELBOURNE AUCKLAND JOHANNESBURG BLANTYRE GABORONE IBADAN PORTSMOUTH NH (USA) CHICAGO

Designed by M2 Graphic Design
Indexed by Indexing Specialists
Originated by Ambassador Litho Ltd.
Printed in Hong Kong/China

06 05 04 03 02
10 9 8 7 6 5 4 3 2 1

ISBN 0 431 14494 X

British Library Cataloguing in Publication Data
Wales, Jenny
A citizen's guide to the economy
1. Great Britain – Economic conditions – 1997 – Juvenile literature
2. Great Britain – Economic policy – 1997 – Juvenile literature
I. Title II. The economy
330.9'41'086

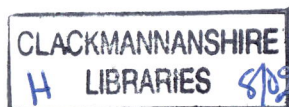

Acknowledgements
The Publishers would like to thank the following for permission to reproduce photographs:
BP Publicity p30; Cameron Balloons p24; Corbis pp6, 17, 32, 39, 43; Format/Melanie Friend p35; Impact/Candy Johnston p5; Janine
Wiedel Photolibrary p13; John Walmsley Photography p14; Report Digital pp15, 40; REPP p38; Rex Features pp9, 36; Telegraph Colour
Library pp19, 26; The *Independent* p22; Tony Stone p16.

Cover photograph reproduced with permission of Tudor Photography.

Every effort has been made to contact copyright holders of any material reproduced in this book.
Any omissions will be rectified in subsequent printings if notice is given to the Publisher.

CONTENTS

Any words appearing in the text in bold, **like this**, are explained in the Glossary.

THE MONEY-GO ROUND

It's your vote

MORE JOBS

MORE MONEY FOR SCHOOLS

CUT TAXES

Keep prices down

New bypasses now

KEEP THE NAVY AFLOAT

MORE POLICEMEN ON THE STREETS

HOSPITAL SPENDING TO RISE

What do you think is important?

If you had to decide what to do for the country, what would you choose? Put the items shown in the headlines into a list. Which of these issues would affect your choice about who should run the country? Why?

When you vote, you choose the political party that you want to see in Parliament for the next five years. But how do you decide? Before an election, all the parties produce a **manifesto** that explains:

>> what they want to do

>> how they plan to raise the money to pay for it all.

Different parties have different lists of things that they think are important. You need to match your list to each manifesto in order to decide whom to vote for.

But you can't have it all! Any political party must decide what it thinks is important, and try to persuade the voters that they are right. When elected, that party must decide how to balance the books. The money to pay for nurses, teachers or new roads must come from **taxes** or borrowing (see page 11). People and businesses pay taxes on the money they earn and the money they spend. The money is then used to pay for the things that the government wants to provide.

For example, if the government decides that cutting unemployment is important, money has to be spent on training the people to fill the jobs that are available.

If low taxes come first, the government has to decide which services will not be provided.

Putting it all together

In deciding how to raise and spend the money, the government is making decisions about how the **economy** is run. The economy is made up of everyone who is spending money, earning money, making things or providing services, like doctors or hairdressers. We are all involved. You and your school friends are part of it, just as much as big businesses and the government. The rest of this book will explain how all these things fit together to make up the economy.

FIND OUT... 🔍 >>

Look at the websites of these main political parties to find out about the things they put at the top of their lists:
www.labour.org.uk
www.conservative.org.uk
www.libdems.org.uk
You might also like to look at some of the other parties, such as
www.greenparty.org.uk.

THE MONEY-GO ROUND
Where does the money come from?

Laura works as a nurse at Kingston Hospital. She earns her living by looking after patients at the hospital. The money that the hospital uses to pay her comes from the government.

Steven works on the assembly line at the Nissan car factory in Sunderland. He earns his living by checking the cars as they reach the end of the line. Nissan pays him with the money it earns from selling cars both in the UK and abroad.

Shakira is a solicitor who works for a small firm in Manchester. She earns her living by helping people with their legal problems. The firm pays her from the fees that the customers pay for the legal advice they receive.

Divyang runs his own business. He earns his living by designing websites for different people. His business is based in a small office in Bristol. He pays himself from the money customers pay him for designing their websites.

People need an income to live. Where does it come from?

People at work

Most people have to earn their living by working. Work can mean all sorts of things. You can work for different sorts of organizations and carry out a wide range of different activities. Laura, Steven, Shakira and Divyang are examples of all these ways of working.

Working for yourself or someone else?

Laura, Steven and Shakira all work for organizations. Divyang works for himself. A growing number of people work for themselves. The pie chart shows the proportion of people in the UK who are employed and those who are self-employed.

**SELF-EMPLOYED
3 MILLION**

**EMPLOYED
23 MILLION**

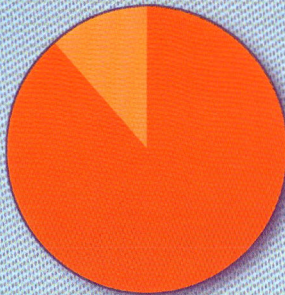

Working for business or government?

Many people, like Laura, are paid by the government, either locally or nationally. Teachers, nurses and policemen are in what is called the public sector where the **taxes** that we pay are used to provide **services**.

Everyone else is in the private sector. This means that they work for businesses that are owned by individuals or groups of people who each own a share of the organization. This pie chart shows the proportion of people who work in the public and private sectors in the UK.

**PUBLIC SECTOR
5 MILLION**

**PRIVATE SECTOR
24 MILLION**

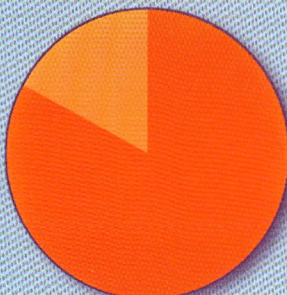

What's the product?

Laura, Shakira and Divyang provide a service. Steven takes part in making things.

More and more people provide a service for others. They may be hairdressers, pilots, policemen, or doctors. They are involved in a wide range of jobs that do not produce 'things'. Any business that sells a product that people can take away with them is a **manufacturing** business. This includes cars, computers, shoes, food and many more products that you will find in the home, office or factory. Together with mining, farming and fishing, these are known as production industries.

**PRODUCTION
INDUSTRIES
5 MILLION**

**SERVICE
INDUSTRIES
18.6 MILLION**

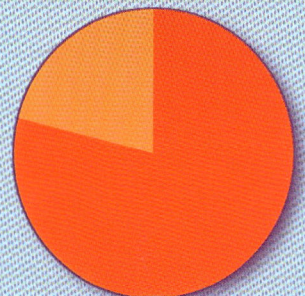

Selling at home and abroad

Steven works for Nissan, a company that manufactures cars. It sells its cars both at home and abroad. When it sells cars to other countries, these cars are known as exports. They bring money into the country.

The money-go-round

All these activities keep money flowing round the **economy**. This is what makes the economy work. People are exchanging their work for payment and then, as you will find out from the next page, spending their earnings.

THE MONEY-GO ROUND
Where does the money go?

Every week Laura, Steven, Shakira and Divyang each go to the supermarket. They spend some of the money they earn on food. While they are there, they may fill their cars with petrol. On Saturday, they sometimes go into town to buy clothes, something for their homes or to have a haircut. The diagram below shows how each of them might spend their pay packet.

They also have to pay all those bills that drop through the letterbox – for using gas, electricity and the telephone. Each one of them will have to pay **council tax** to the local council. This pays for **services** that are provided in the local area.

Before they are paid, **income tax** and **National Insurance** are deducted from their wages by their employers. In Divyang's case, he has to work out himself how much income tax and National Insurance he owes, because he is self-employed.

FIND OUT... 🔍 »

What sort of things do you spend your money on? Which things are services and which are manufactured? Are they made in the UK or in other countries?

Spending money

Every time someone buys something, money changes hands. This may be in the form of notes and coins or by using a **credit card**. The result is the same, as money passes from one person to another.

If Steven buys a pint of milk at the corner shop, he pays in cash. The money helps the shopkeeper to:
» run his shop
» buy the milk from the dairy.

It then helps:
» the dairy to process the milk
» the farmer to keep his cows.

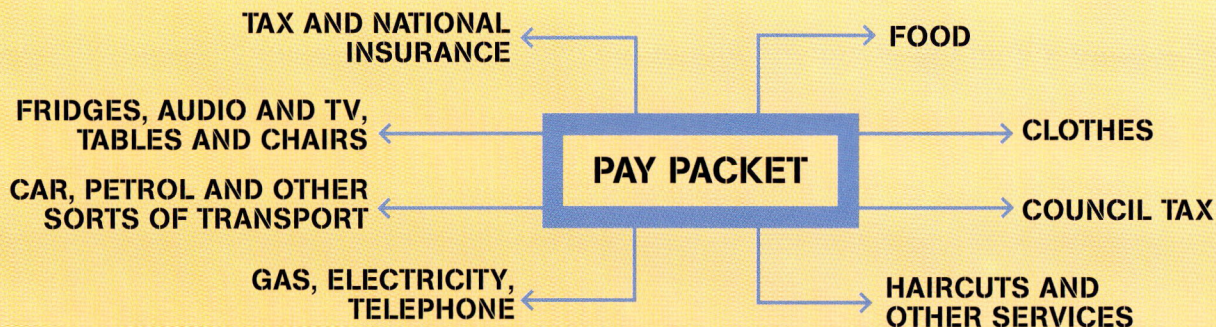

TAX AND NATIONAL INSURANCE → FOOD

FRIDGES, AUDIO AND TV, TABLES AND CHAIRS → CLOTHES

CAR, PETROL AND OTHER SORTS OF TRANSPORT → **PAY PACKET** → COUNCIL TAX

GAS, ELECTRICITY, TELEPHONE → HAIRCUTS AND OTHER SERVICES

If Shakira has her hair cut, she pays the hairdresser using a credit card. The money is used to help the hairdresser:

>> pay the rent on his shop
>> employ other people
>> buy shampoo, towels and all the other things he needs
>> pay himself.

When Laura fills her car with petrol, she pays in cash. The money helps the garage owner to:

>> run his garage
>> buy the petrol from the oil company.

The oil company then uses the money to:

>> help them pump oil from wells
>> process it
>> transport it to the garage.

When Divyang needs a new computer, he buys it from an Internet site that gives him a good price. He pays with a credit card. The money helps the business to:

>> keep its website going and employ staff
>> buy the computer from the manufacturer
>> deliver the computer to Divyang.

The computer manufacturer uses the money that it receives from the Internet computer sales company to help:

>> run its factory
>> buy the parts it needs to build computers
>> employ people.

When Divyang looks at the back of his computer he finds that it was made in Korea, on the other side of the world. It is an **import**. Many things we buy are made in other countries. This gives us more choice about what we can buy. Some places can make things more cheaply than others, so if we buy their products our money goes further.

Money makes the world go round

All these examples show how money flows round the **economy**. When we buy things, money passes from one person to another in exchange for our purchases. It is then passed on again in every **transaction** that is made. These exchanges keep the economy running, keep people employed and give us food to eat, clothes to wear and all the other things we want or need.

When people buy these disk drives, the money helps to keep the business running.

FIND OUT... 🔍 >>

Pick an item that you have bought recently and work out the chain that brought it to you.

>>

9

THE MONEY-GO ROUND
Where does the government get its money?

Laura, the nurse, pays **taxes** in all sorts of ways.

She pays:

>> **Income tax** and **National Insurance** which are deducted from her pay

>> Value added tax (VAT) on most of the things she buys

>> Car tax when she buys a new car

>> Petrol tax on every litre

>> Excise duty on a bottle of wine, a beer or a packet of cigarettes.

Paying taxes

We all pay taxes so that the government can provide the range of **services** that we need. The taxes come in different forms so that they spread over the things we do and buy.

>> Value added tax is paid on almost everything we buy apart from food, children's clothes, books and newspapers. We all pay the same amount, however much we earn. This means that it is a **regressive tax**, as the poor pay as much as the rich.

>> Income tax is not paid by people who earn very little, but as your income rises, you pay more tax. It is worked out as a percentage of your earnings. People on higher wages start to pay a

higher percentage of their earnings. It is a **progressive tax** because people who earn more, pay more. (Why do you think this is? Is it fair?) National Insurance is paid in the same way.

>> Excise duty is charged on a special range of items, many of which are not very good for us if we have too much. These include alcohol and cigarettes.

>> Other taxes include those on cars and petrol. A tax generally puts up the price of a product. Some taxes are raised in the local area. These include **council tax** and **business rates** (see page 14).

This pie chart shows how the tax we pay is divided up.

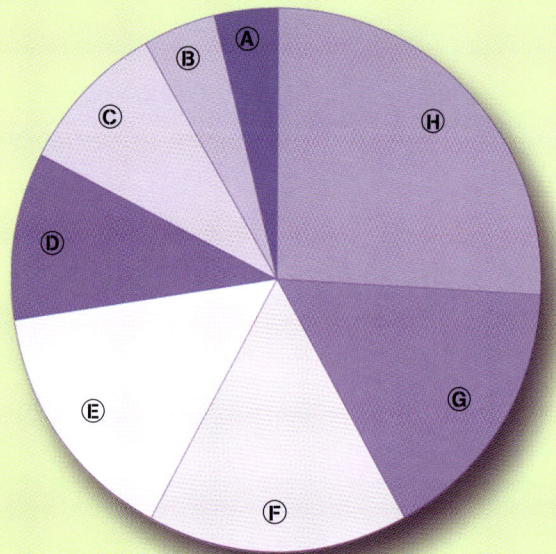

Ⓐ COUNCIL TAX	Ⓔ OTHER
Ⓑ BUSINESS RATES	Ⓕ NATIONAL INSURANCE
Ⓒ CORPORATION TAX	Ⓖ VAT
Ⓓ EXCISE DUTY	Ⓗ INCOME TAX

Businesses pay taxes, too

Divyang runs a website design business. He has set up his own company, which means that he trades under its name instead of his own. The company has to pay **corporation tax** on the profits that it makes. Divyang adds up all the money the business makes and subtracts all the costs of running the business, including the amount he pays himself. He then has to pay tax on what money is left. All companies pay taxes. The table below shows how much some famous companies pay in tax.

The big payers!

COMPANY	WHAT DOES IT DO?	HOW MUCH TAX DID IT PAY?
BP	OILS AND CHEMICALS	£259 MILLION
TESCO	SUPERMARKETS	£259 MILLION
PILKINGTONS	GLASS AND TILES	£48 MILLION
ARRIVA	TRANSPORT	£44 MILLION
NORTHERN FOODS	FOOD PRODUCTION	£18 MILLION
AMSTRAD	COMPUTING	£4 MILLION

Why tax?

The government wants to raise money, or **revenue**, from taxation. It uses it for health, education, roads, defence and many other things. It may also want to persuade us to buy less of some things.

When the price of a product goes up, we often buy less of it, so if the government wants us to reduce the amount we smoke, drink or drive our cars, a tax increase may help. Sometimes, however, we want things so much that we go on buying them, whatever the price.

Making ends meet

Just like everyone else, if the government wants to spend more than its income, it has to borrow. When it borrows, it has to pay **interest** to the people who lend it money.

The amount that a government needs to borrow depends on all sorts of things. It may have planned to spend more, or events may have happened which made spending bigger than was planned.

The decisions on taxes and spending are announced once a year in the **Budget**. The Chancellor of the Exchequer is responsible for deciding where the money comes from and how it is spent. He works with the government departments, like health, education and transport, to decide what is needed and what must come first.

THE MONEY-GO ROUND
How the government spends its money

"THERE'S GOING TO BE A NEW BY-PASS AT LAST"

"YOU SHOULD SEE THE NEW IT CENTRE AT ROSELAND SCHOOL"

"I'M JUST GOING TO COLLECT GRAN'S PENSION FOR HER"

"JOE'S BEEN ON UNEMPLOYMENT BENEFIT FOR TWO YEARS NOW"

"HELP! WE'VE BEEN BURGLED. CALL THE POLICE"

All these comments refer to things that the government pays for. The government spends its money on a wide range of products and **services**. It also gives some to people in the form of **pensions** and **benefits**. This pie chart shows just where the money goes.

FIND OUT...

The Treasury is the government department that is responsible for the Budget. Have a look at its website, www.treasury.gov.uk, to find out how the government raises and spends its money. Click on the 'Budget' heading on the site. You will find a summary document that explains about the government's spending decisions.

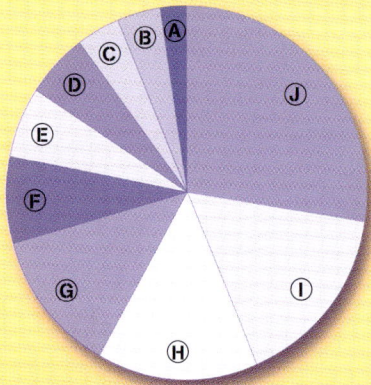

Ⓐ TRANSPORT	Ⓕ DEBT INTEREST
Ⓑ HOUSING & ENVIRONMENT	Ⓖ EDUCATION
Ⓒ INDUSTRY, AGRICULTURE AND EMPLOYMENT	Ⓗ NHS
Ⓓ LAW AND ORDER	Ⓘ OTHER EXPENDITURE
Ⓔ DEFENCE	Ⓙ SOCIAL SECURITY

Why does the government spend?

Just think of a world without all the things that the government pays for. Some of those things might be provided by businesses, but others would be a problem because it would be hard to persuade people to pay for them.

Won't pay!

What is the response if someone's house has been burgled? Call the police! How could a police force be organized if the government did not provide it?

Would it work if people paid a business to run the police? What would happen if you didn't pay? Would you not be protected from football hooligans or terrorists?

This is one area that is difficult to provide unless provided for everyone, so governments usually organize it. Defence and roads are usually in the same category. In some countries, motorways are run by businesses, but the rest of the roads are provided by the state.

Can't pay!

If education and health were only available to people who had enough money to pay for them, many people would be forced to go without. Both services are available in the private sector, but are often very expensive. The government provides them, so that everyone can be educated, and looked after when they are ill.

Making these services available to everyone is not just a matter of looking after the whole population. If people suffer from ill-health and lack education, they are less productive and unable to achieve their potential. They might find it difficult to find and keep a job, so the state would have to look after them. The government then has to pay them benefits. Saving on health and education may result in spending money in other areas later.

How much?

Governments always argue about how much they will spend. We hear all about 'Cuts' and 'More spending' at election times. Over the years, there has been a steady increase in the amount the government spends. At the moment, it amounts to about £6,000 for each person, each year. Our voting decisions often depend on what the political parties say that they will do about **taxes** and spending if they win the election.

The government builds new hospitals and schools. This is the new maternity unit at St Thomas's Hospital in London.

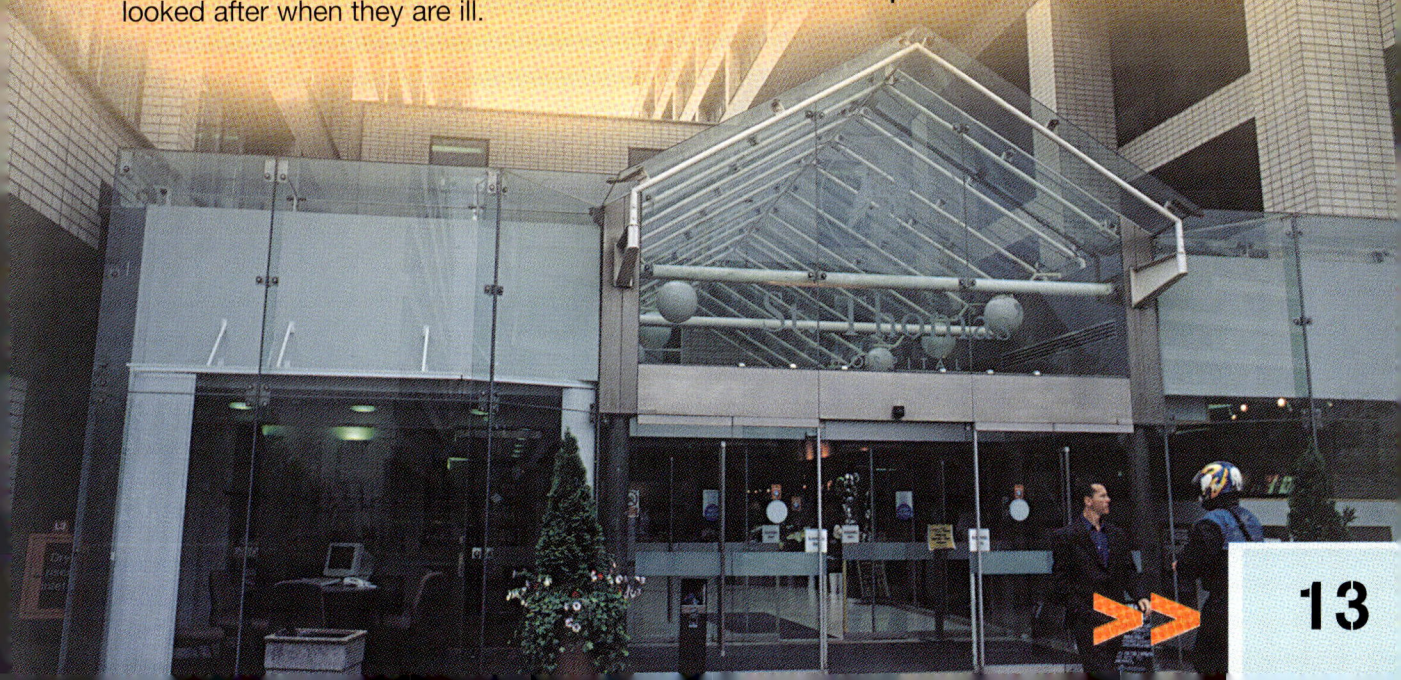

THE MONEY-GO ROUND
The local budget

Your local council is responsible for education and a range of other services for your community. These include **social services**, leisure, planning and transport, housing, fire and police.

The amount of that the local council spends will depend on all sorts of things. Here are some examples:

>> If the population of the area is very young, they will need lots of schools

>> If there are many old people, social services will be in demand

>> If there are lots of people, there will be lots of rubbish to collect.

A brand new school, for example, is a very expensive item and has to be paid for from **taxes**. The council will work out how much it needs to spend in the coming year, and then calculate how much it must raise from taxes. While doing this, it must always consider the amount of money that will be available to spend.

The council has to work out its priorities. It never has the money to provide everything it would like to. Central government does not give the local council a free hand, because it sets a limit on how much money can be spent.

Science equipment and computers are expensive items needed by schools.

Who pays?

The local council raises money from residents and businesses in the area in the following ways:

>> **Council tax** is paid by all the residents of the area. The amount that each person pays will depend on the value of the house they live in. So, people who live in big houses will pay more than those who live in small houses.

>> **Business rates** are paid by all the local businesses. The amount that is paid depends on the rent that could be charged for the office, shop or factory that the business uses.

Money from council tax and business rates help pay for local, council-run leisure centres and swimming pools.

Money also comes from central government. The amount depends on the needs of the area and how much can be raised locally. Poor areas tend to receive more than rich areas of the country.

If many people are unemployed in a certain area, houses will tend to have a lower value, so the council tax will only bring in a relatively small amount of money. On the other side of the coin, people in these areas often need a lot of help from social services, so spending will be higher.

Who decides?

Your local council is elected by all the voters in the area. The political parties that put up candidates are mostly the same as in national elections. In some cases there may be candidates who stand for election on the basis of a particular local issue.

When you vote in local elections, you are helping to decide what happens where you live. If you don't vote, you can't complain about the decisions the council makes!

FIND OUT...

How does your local council raise and spend its money? You can find out from the town hall, council offices or the library. The council might also have a website that will tell you what is going on, as well.

KEEPING CONTROL
Too much money?

Must have ...

Every year, the lucky producer of the 'must have' Christmas present faces the same dilemma. Whether it is a computer game, a doll or a toy from the latest film, every child in the country wants one. Stocks run out and it's often impossible to get more into the shops in time. Parents are prepared to pay anything to ensure that happy smiling face on Christmas morning, so very often the price of the product goes up.

Pushing up prices

This is just one small example of the way prices can rise. Just imagine what happens when people get more wealthy. The more money they have, the more they want and the more they are prepared to pay for all sorts of things. If there is not enough of a certain thing to go round, the price will go up even more as people compete to buy the product.

When this happens across the country, the general level of prices rises and we have **inflation.**

Sometimes inflation can happen because the cost of raw materials for making things goes up. The price of oil affects the cost of almost everything we buy. Oil is used to make plastics. It is hard to think of products that don't need plastic. Oil is turned into petrol so delivery costs will go up. Also we do not seem to be able to do without petrol, and are prepared to pay a higher price for it.

Inflation happens because:

>> we have more money to spend so are prepared to pay higher prices

>> the cost of making things goes up and we are prepared to go on buying them at a higher price.

What's the problem?

A little inflation is the normal state of affairs. The government aims for about 2%. This means that the value of our money falls by 2% each year as prices rise. Sometimes things get really out of hand. In the 1970s, inflation reached 23%, so each year everyone's money was worth nearly a quarter less than the year before.

In some countries inflation has reached 300%! This causes chaos, as people don't want to hold money as it soon becomes worthless. They start to barter or exchange goods instead.

Who's affected?

Inflation is a real problem for some people:

>> Do you know anyone who is retired and living on a **pension**? They may well be worried about inflation if their pension payments are fixed at the same amount of money. If inflation is high, their pension payments will buy less and less each year.

>> Any business that **exports** its products will be worried by inflation. If there is more inflation in the UK, people in other countries will not want to buy from here because the prices will be higher.

But inflation can be good for others:

>> If you own a house, its selling price will rise when there is inflation.

>> If you have borrowed money, its value will fall, because the amount you have to pay back shrinks if your income goes up as much as inflation.

Spending made easy

When people become too confident about the future they begin to use the plastic cards in their wallets too frequently.

Credit cards certainly make life easy. You can use them to buy things and then pay later. It is important to remember that if the bill is not paid in full straight away, you have to pay **interest** on the amount that is left.

Credit card spending is one thing that the government looks at when it is trying to forecast the pattern of inflation.

Why do rising fuel prices make other things more expensive?

TEXACO

THE NATIONAL LOTTERY

24 Hours
Mini Market

Unleaded Litre **82.9**

Diesel Litre **83.9**

4 Star LRP 4 Litre **86.9**

KEEPING CONTROL
Keeping prices under control

"I LIKE THE BRITISH MODEL BUT IT'S SO EXPENSIVE. I THINK I'LL HAVE TO BUY THE ONE THAT'S MADE IN AMERICA"

"I'VE MANAGED ON MY PENSION FOR ALL THESE YEARS, BUT RISING PRICES MEAN IT DOESN'T GO SO FAR"

Why worry?

Inflation causes concern for all sorts of people, so the government generally tries to keep it under control. The quotes above show how inflation makes life difficult.

If prices in the UK rise:

>> people at home will be tempted to buy products from other countries

>> people abroad will stop buying UK products.

If this happens, there will be fewer jobs in the country so unemployment will rise.

Rising unemployment and the falling value of **pensions** make people very unhappy. As changes like this persuade people to vote for a different party at election time, governments tend to worry about them.

What can be done?

Interest rates are most commonly used to control inflation. Putting up the price of borrowing money persuades people to borrow less. If people borrow less, they spend less. If they spend less, prices won't be pushed up, so inflation will be steadied.

It also affects people who already have a **loan**, as the repayments will be more expensive, so they will have less to spend on other things.

Who makes the decision?

Governments are often accused of wanting to make people better off just before an election, in the hope that they will win votes. This often results in inflation after the election as everyone has had more to spend. To prevent this short-term approach, decisions about changes in interest rates were put into the hands of a group of people at the **Bank of England**, which looks after the country's money. This group is known as the **Monetary Policy Committee**.

The Bank of England helps to control inflation.

Deciding what to do

The Monetary Policy Committee is made up of people who work full time at the Bank of England, and others who are economic experts from outside. They are given information about all the changes that are taking place in the **economy**. This helps them to decide whether interest rates should go up, go down or stay the same.

These are just a few of the things that the committee needs to know:

>> Are wages going up?

>> Are prices going up?

>> Are we **importing** more from other countries?

>> Are we **exporting** more to other countries?

>> Are we borrowing more from the banks?

>> Are more people unemployed?

>> Can businesses find enough people with the right skills?

What happens next?

When the Monetary Policy Committee has made its decision, it affects all the interest rates in the country. Often banks and building societies change their interest rates straight away. Sometimes, if the changes are small, the rates might not change immediately.

>> **19**

KEEPING CONTROL
Without a job?

"I'VE JUST LEFT SCHOOL AND THERE ARE NO JOBS ROUND HERE. MY DAD'S UNEMPLOYED, TOO. I'VE GOT A FEW GCSEs BUT THERE DOESN'T SEEM ANY POINT IN STAYING AT SCHOOL, IT WON'T MAKE ANY DIFFERENCE"

"I LEARNT A TRADE WHEN I LEFT SCHOOL, BUT EVERYTHING'S CHANGED AND THEY DON'T NEED ME ANYMORE. I'LL HAVE TO GO BACK TO COLLEGE AND RETRAIN IF I'M GOING TO GET ANOTHER JOB"

"I WISH I'D GONE ON TO COLLEGE. ALL THE JOBS ARE FOR PEOPLE WITH SKILLS"

"I'M JUST TOO OLD. EVERYONE WANTS TO EMPLOY YOUNG PEOPLE"

Who is unemployed?

People are unemployed for all sorts of reasons, but some groups have more difficulty finding work than others. The quotes above represent some of these groups.

Where do you live?

In some parts of the country, jobs are harder to find than in other parts. This is often because businesses have closed down. It may be because their products are no longer wanted or can be made more cheaply elsewhere.

Have you got the right skill?

There are lots of jobs for people with IT skills, but few for those in the steel industry or mining. Having the right skills for today is a good way to make sure you have a job.

What are your qualifications?

People with more qualifications usually find jobs more easily. It is much harder for people who leave school with no qualifications to find a job.

How old are you?

Businesses seem to want to employ younger people. People who lose their jobs when they are close to retirement age often struggle to find new employment. Age isn't the only source of **discrimination**. People may suffer discrimination on grounds of race, sex or religion, even though this is against the law.

>>

money and buying all sorts of products. Lots of people are then employed to make the products and provide the **services**.

In a slump, people buy less because they are scared of being unemployed. When people buy less, the number of jobs falls because fewer people are needed to make the products and provide the services.

The government tries to smooth the pattern of booms and slumps.

Does it matter?

There are three main reasons why it's important to keep **unemployment figures** low:

>> Most people are unhappy if they don't have a job. They can't provide for themselves and their families. They are more likely to be ill and the children's education can suffer. All this makes it harder to find another job, and the children may be disadvantaged.

>> If people do not have a job, their skills are being wasted. People who are employed make things or provide a service that is sold. They are contributing to the economy. If many people are unemployed, the country's output will be lower.

>> Unemployment is expensive. Almost everyone who is unemployed receives **benefits**. The more people who are unemployed, the higher the bill will be. These benefits are paid out of **taxes**. If taxes are used for benefits, they cannot be used for all the other things that the government provides.

UK REGIONAL UNEMPLOYMENT, 2001

7.6%	Scotland	6.2%	West Midlands
9.1%	North East	5.1%	East Midlands
7.0%	Northern Ireland	3.6%	Eastern
6.0%	Yorkshire and the Humber	7.0%	London
5.3%	North West	3.3%	South East
6.1%	Wales	4.1%	South West

Booms and slumps

The number of people who are unemployed will vary from time to time. A booming **economy** means that people are spending

KEEPING CONTROL
In search of a job?

Sean had left school, thinking there was little point in staying on, as there were no jobs where he lived. One evening, his dad came in with the local paper. They spread open the jobs pages on the kitchen table. At the same moment they both spotted the full-page advert for jobs at the new call centre that a bank was about to open nearby.

They needed all sorts of people – not just people to answer the phones, but others to run the canteens, look after the buildings and keep all the computers working. Training was on offer as well. Sean and his dad rushed to the phone and arranged to go in for the open day. At last there was a chance that they might get jobs.

At work in a call centre – these people deal with incoming calls.

A helping hand

Getting people into work is often important for governments. There are several ways of approaching the problem.

>> Help for businesses.
Sean, in the case story on page 22, lives in a part of the country where many people are unemployed. What that area needs most of all is for businesses to move in and provide jobs. The bank had probably been persuaded to build its call centre there because the government helped by providing money. There are grants available for areas of high unemployment. The government can also give help to business in order to train people.

>> Help with training.
Sean also needs training. He had left school at sixteen and had no special skills to help him get a job. In his case, the business was offering to train people. Governments often have schemes to help people get the training they need. These aim to provide people with skills in new areas, to update skills or develop existing skills.

>> Help for everyone.
Some people have difficulty getting a job because of **discrimination**. In order to try to make things fair, there are laws that prevent businesses from discriminating against people because of their sex, race or religion. Businesses are also expected to employ a number of disabled people.

>> Helping the **economy**.
Unemployment can result from the economy 'slowing down'. Everyone spends less, so businesses don't need as many people to provide the things that we all buy. If the government spends more or reduces the amount it takes in tax, it leaves more for us to spend. If we have more to spend, we buy more and therefore businesses will employ people to make the things we want.

The **Monetary Policy Committee**, which decides on the level of **interest rates**, must think about the effect that any change will have on the economy as a whole. If they make it more expensive for people to borrow money, spending will be reduced and this can make unemployment worse.

Because unemployment varies across the country, it can be difficult for the people on this committee to decide what to do. In order to reduce **inflation** in some parts of the country, they may make unemployment worse in others.

FIND OUT...

What schemes are available to help people improve their training? Have a look at the website of the Department of Education and Skills www.dfes.gov.uk. You can also find out from your local Job Centre.
Also, have a look at the websites of the different political parties (see box on page 5), and find out about their policies on unemployment. What do you think of them?

>> **23**

PART 3

WHAT ABOUT BUSINESS?
What does business do?

Cameron Balloons

Standing at the factory door, you will see all sorts of things going in. Bales of special fabric, baskets, burners, packaging and much more, are all part of making hot air balloons. People arrive through another door. Their contribution is very important, as they are responsible for putting all these materials together to meet the customers' requirements. Inside the factory, there are machines and various types of special equipment that the staff use to make the balloons.

Putting it all together

Businesses use a range of **resources** to make products. The resources will vary greatly from one business to another. A farm, for example, is quite simple. If it is producing crops, it uses the ground, seeds, fertilizers, machinery and people. A car factory uses many more resources. They buy in steel, electrical machinery, wheels, and so on from other businesses, and then put them all together using people, robots and equipment.

This process means that a business will experience **added value**. The business literally adds value to all the resources by putting them together. It can sell the end product at a price that is higher than the cost of all the resources added together.

FIND OUT...

To find out more about how the hot air balloon manufacturer Cameron Balloons adds value, have a look at Virtual Worlds on www.bized.ac.uk where you can explore the way the business works.

What's the product?

The examples so far have all been things that you can see and touch. Many businesses, however, produce **services**. Solicitors, plumbers, estate agents, dentists and banks all provide a service. Pages 6–7 explain how people earn a living in service industries.

These businesses add value in just the same way. They buy resources that are used in the process. People are, of course, very important in service industries. They often meet the public and therefore need special skills, as customers can be very demanding. The service is sold to the public at a higher price than the cost of all the resources.

Finance for business

A small business can be set up very easily. A hairdresser who wants to set up a business travelling to people's homes just needs a bag of equipment and an advert in the local paper. This will not cost very much, and can often be financed by the individual.

Opening a salon would be more expensive. The hairdresser might need to borrow money from friends or relatives to do this. The bank might also help out.

Another strategy would be to set up a private company and sell shares to people. A private company is a formal way of sharing ownership. The **shareholders** are limited in number and will expect to receive a return on the money that they have put into the business. You can identify a private company because it has the letters 'Ltd' (an abbreviation of 'Limited') after its name.

When a business starts to grow, it may need more money to expand than is available from the small group of private shareholders. It can then become a public company that sells shares to the general public. Almost all the famous names, such as BP, Barclays Bank, Tesco and Granada are public companies. You will notice that these businesses have 'plc' (an abbreviation of 'public limited company') after their names. Their shares are bought and sold on the **Stock Exchange**.

Remember...

Business is risky. No one can make people buy the products of a business! If you set up in business yourself, or put money into someone else's, you may make money – but you might also lose it.

FIND OUT...

Have a look at the financial pages of a newspaper, or its website. You will see the value of the shares of all the major companies. If you follow them for a while, you can see how their value changes. This often tells you how well the business is doing.

WHAT ABOUT BUSINESS?
Why run a business?

Divyang designs websites. He used to work for a big company, but left to set up his own business. When asked why, he answered:

" I like the independence it gives me. I can work when I want to, as long as I meet the deadlines for customers. I know that if I produce good websites, the word will spread and the business will grow. It's all down to me. I have to be responsible for organizing everything, but I don't have anyone telling me what to do.

I'm earning less at the moment than I was in the big company, but the business is growing quite quickly. Anyway, it's worth the risk. I like being my own boss. "

What's the motive?

People's instant answer to the question 'Why run a business?' is 'To make money'.

Many people who actually run their own businesses would answer differently. They enjoy the independence, and may be prepared to sacrifice some **profit** in order to be in charge of their activities. If the business is to keep going, however, making a profit is important. Every business has to keep track of the **costs** of running the business and the **revenue** that it earned from selling the products.

> Would you like to run your own business or work for someone else? Why?

Bigger businesses have to be concerned about making a profit because their **shareholders** expect a return on the money that they have put into the business. They often have other objectives, too:

>> To grow and make more profit.
Many businesses aim to grow. They have to be careful not to let costs rise too fast, as this will reduce profit.

>> To increase sales and become a well-known name.
Becoming a well-known name can persuade people to buy the product, but selling more can increase costs. A new shop, for example, can be expensive.

>> To keep prices low to compete with other businesses.
Some businesses sell products that are made by many others. Low prices are one way that you can persuade people to buy your products.

>> To survive when things get difficult.
If there is a lot of unemployment, people often buy less. A business then has to work hard to make enough profit and survive.

>> To look after the environment.
Many businesses are involved in activities that might harm the environment. They often want to show people how careful they are.

>> To keep a good image.
Businesses have become aware that having a bad image is not good for sales. They will work hard to make sure that their image is not damaged.

There are other objectives, too, as all businesses are different. Sometimes people just want a quiet life and, once things seem to be running smoothly, let the business run itself. This can be a dangerous strategy, as there is almost always someone who is looking for an opportunity. Customers can disappear overnight if everyone is not alert.

FIND OUT...

Support is available from the government and other bodies for people who want to start up and run their own businesses.

Have a look at the websites for The Prince's Trust, www.prince's-trust.org.uk and The Small Business Service, www.sbs.gov.uk

WHAT ABOUT BUSINESS?
Business across the world

Nike makes and sells sports clothes and shoes in many countries around the world. In order to compete with other brands, it builds factories in places where costs are low. Many are in countries like Thailand and Vietnam where wages are low, and running a factory is cheap compared with the USA or Europe.

Nike's products are available in almost every country. The advertising usually focuses on famous sports personalities who people like to be associated with. Nike will alter the advertising to appeal to people in different countries. It is a **multinational** business.

A bigger business

The world is now a very small place. The same brands of clothes, computers, cars and many other things appear in almost every country. To make the most of this enormous market place, some businesses have expanded into other countries. This allows them to grow and make more **profits**. The aim can be to serve the world market more efficiently. Sometimes you need a factory near where you sell the products. Food, for example, can't always travel very far.

Like Nike, many businesses are looking for places with low **costs** so that they can compete with others who make similar products. Electronic communications make things even easier.

Some businesses employ computer programmers in India, for example, as wages are much lower than in Europe.

Best behaviour?

Multinationals are often challenged about how they treat people who make their products in the developing world. In a company's search for low costs, people may be expected to work very long hours. Sometimes, even children are employed.

In Europe and the USA, there are laws to protect people in the workplace, but even here it can be difficult to make sure that everyone keeps them. In the developing world, even when there are laws, they are difficult to enforce.

Businesses are often concerned about their image. Customers can quickly be put off products by stories in the newspapers and on television that suggest that people are being treated badly. Many multinationals have programmes that lay down rules for their suppliers in the developing world. It can, however, still be difficult to monitor people who run the factories that make their products.

Making a judgement

When stories hit the headlines telling us about child labour and low wages, we have to put the facts into context. It is often much more complicated than it seems. There is no excuse for treating people badly

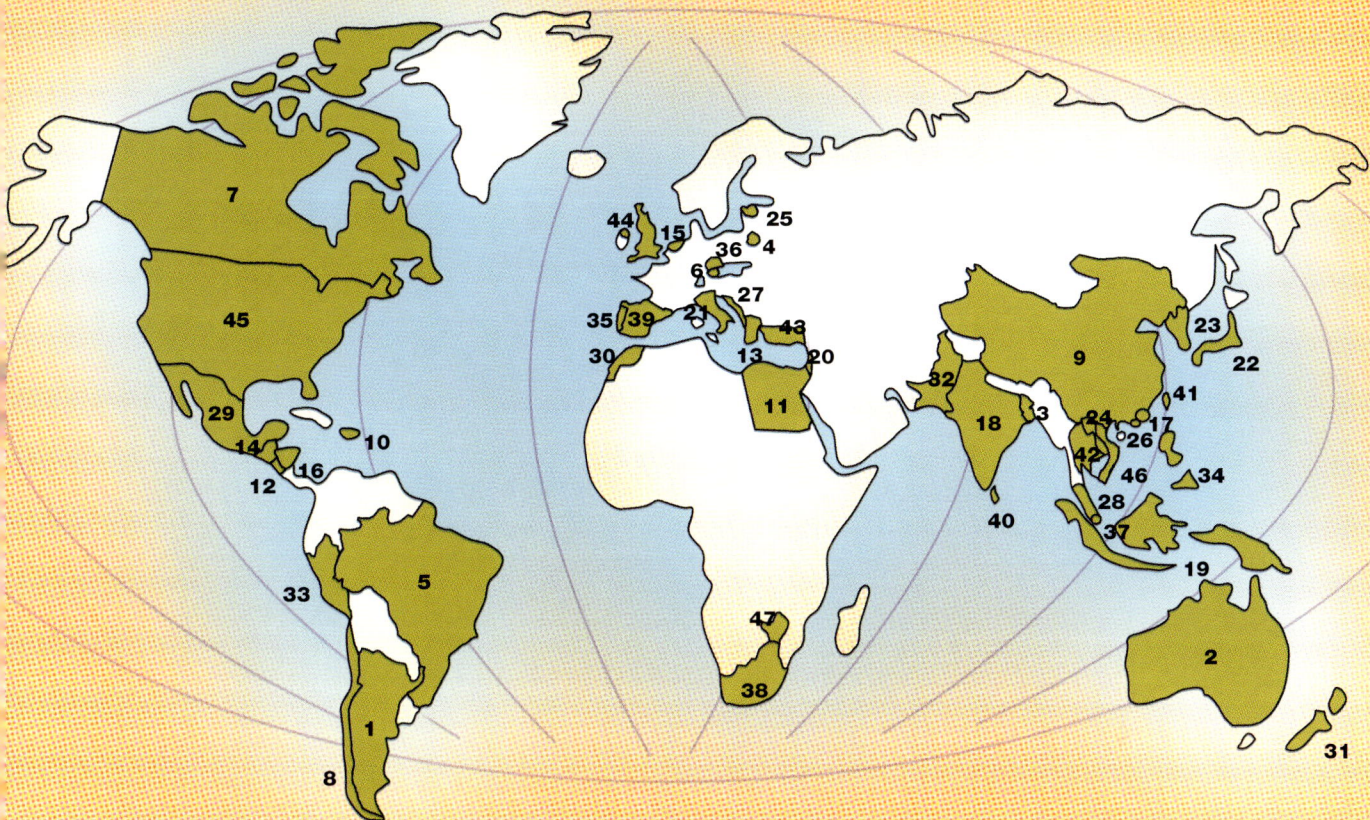

1) ARGENTINA	10) DOMINICAN REPUBLIC	19) INDONESIA	29) MEXICO	39) SPAIN
2) AUSTRALIA	11) EGYPT	20) ISRAEL	30) MOROCCO	40) SRI LANKA
3) BANGLADESH	12) EL SALVADOR	21) ITALY	31) NEW ZEALAND	41) TAIWAN
4) BELARUS	13) GREECE	22) JAPAN	32) PAKISTAN	42) THAILAND
5) BRAZIL	14) GUATEMALA	23) KOREA	33) PERU	43) TURKEY
6) BULGARIA	15) HOLLAND	24) LAOS	34) PHILIPPINES	44) UK
7) CANADA	16) HONDURAS	25) LITHUANIA	35) PORTUGAL	45) USA
8) CHILE	17) HONG KONG	26) MACAU	36) ROMANIA	46) VIETNAM
9) CHINA	18) INDIA	27) MACEDONIA	37) SINGAPORE	47) ZIMBABWE
		28) MALAYSIA	38) SOUTH AFRICA	

Nike is an international company and produces goods in all the places marked on the map.

and making them work long hours, seven days a week, but other situations may need a closer look.

In countries where there are no **benefits** for the unemployed, people without work can starve. Sometimes, a child who is working can keep a family alive. Even organizations working to help people in developing countries do not always condemn child labour.

Another factor is that wage levels in many countries are lower than in Europe. You may have noticed this if you have been on holiday to countries where your money goes further than in the UK. You need to know how the wages being paid compare with the country's average wages before you can make a judgement.

FIND OUT...

What can you do to make sure that you only buy things that are made by people who are being treated fairly? Have a look at the Fairtrade Foundation's website, www.fairtrade.co.uk. The links from this website tell you about businesses that ensure that producers are treated fairly, and about other organizations that campaign for fair trade practices.

WHAT ABOUT BUSINESS?
Good citizens in business?

BP at Wilton has been working alongside Spike the Hedgehog to teach road safety to primary children in the Wilton and Redcar regions. 'Walk to School Week' in May 2000 was supported by BP, who provided children with fluorescent vests and a road safety pack. In partnership with Redcar and Cleveland Borough Council, BP also helped to produce a road safety training video.

BP, the oil and chemicals business, runs programmes for schools across the country. It focuses on schools near its plants in places like Hull, South Wales and Scotland. Staff from the oil refinery or chemical works go into schools to help in all sorts of ways. The road safety activities are just one example of the sort of work that goes on.

BP, along with Spike the Hedgehog, is helping the community by encouraging road safety.

Win/win

Businesses affect the lives of many people. These include their staff, customers, suppliers, **shareholders** and the community in general. By looking after these groups, a business can build good relationships, which help them to work more efficiently because:

>> Staff will work with more commitment

>> Suppliers will ensure that orders are delivered on time

>> Customers will be happy to go on buying the products

>> Shareholders will want to keep their shares

>> The community will understand what the business is doing.

These groups are known as **stakeholders** because they all have a stake in the business. The diagram below shows the links.

A business that works carefully to ensure that all the stakeholders are well looked after and know what is going on will benefit. This is often called a win/win situation because everyone gains.

SUPPLIERS

CUSTOMERS

THE BUSINESS

OWNERS AND SHAREHOLDERS

EMPLOYEES

COMMUNITY

FIND OUT...

Have a look at the websites of some large businesses. Find out how they work with the community. Try www.bp.com or www.unilever.com. As these two companies are multinationals, you will also be able to see how they work with stakeholders around the world.

Not just for big business

In your local area, businesses help all sorts of organizations. Scout groups, music groups, schools and many others often benefit. They do all sorts of things from providing work experience placements to supporting the raffle at the Summer Fête. You may even see rubbish bins that are sponsored by local businesses.

All these activities help everyone to consider that the business makes a real contribution to the community. They aim to give people a positive attitude towards the business.

What about the environment?

Many businesses have an impact on the environment. Because of the nature of the product, it may be impossible to prevent damage taking place. As a result, it is important to explain what is happening and how the impact is being reduced. Websites are often used to let people know what is going on.

Businesses have realized how important it is to think about the effect of their actions and keep people informed. For example, many now work with Greenpeace, the environmental campaigning organization. Greenpeace offers advice to help businesses to get things right. This prevents bad press in newspapers if businesses are accused of causing damage.

> There is probably a range of businesses that help your school or other groups that you belong to. What does each business do to help? How does its help affect your view of the business?

WHERE DO I FIT IN?

What shall I buy?

Bill Gates, who set up Microsoft, is worth billions of dollars. He has built his own house with every technological gadget that you can imagine – and many more that you can't! Pictures on the wall are created electronically, so when he is fed up with the work of one artist, he can see some new ones at the press of a button. He has every sort of music, wherever he goes in the house.

Bill Gates spent more than $60 million on building his home in Washington, USA.

Making choices

Bill Gates can buy anything he wants. Most of us can't. We have to make choices. Our income, whether it is from working, **pensions**, benefits or pocket money, doesn't go as far as we would like. In other words, we have a limited budget.

How do we choose?

If you have been given some money for your birthday, how do you decide what to buy? You might want some new trainers – but which pair?

You might think about:

>> The price

>> The brand

>> The design

>> What's in fashion

>> Anything else you want

>> How much you have to spend.

If you really want the most fashionable brand, you may be prepared to pay the highest price. On the other hand, you might want to buy something else as well. If this is the case, then you might compromise and buy a cheaper pair.

Whatever the decision, we go through the same process, whether we realize it or not. Buying a pair of trainers is quite a simple choice really! Just think about the sort of decisions that the average family has to make every week.

The priorities for a family have to be a roof over its head, food and clothing. These necessities are at the top of the list. The tighter the budget, the harder the choices.

Changing choices?

As time goes by, the list of things that people buy changes. There are many reasons for this, including:

>> New things are being invented

>> Fashion changes

>> Prices change

>> People have more to spend.

But some things on people's lists don't change. The basic things like milk, bread, and petrol continue to be on the list because they are things that we cannot do without. Every now and again, something goes wrong and there is a shortage of one of these products and so the price of the product goes through the roof. What happens? We continue to buy because we really need it.

Not enough?

Because almost everything has a price, some people find it difficult to buy the things they need. The old, the unemployed and people on very low incomes are helped by the **benefits** from the state. The **taxes** we pay are used to help people in this way (look at page 12–13).

Adding it all up

All parts of the economy spend money:

>> People spend the money they earn

>> Businesses spend the money they earn

>> Governments spend the money they raise in taxes.

This is how money flows round the **economy**. When we buy and sell things to other countries, money flows between countries as well. **Imports** take money out and **exports** bring money in.

WHERE DO I FIT IN?
Spend or save?

"IF I REALLY WANT THOSE TROUSERS, I'M GOING TO HAVE TO SAVE OVER THE NEXT FEW WEEKS"

"I WANT TO GO ON HOLIDAY WITH MY FRIENDS NEXT SUMMER, SO I'VE GOT TO SAVE AS MUCH AS I CAN"

"I LOVE THAT CAR, BUT I'LL HAVE TO SAVE UP FOR IT"

"WE ARE SAVING UP TO PUT DOWN A DEPOSIT ON A HOUSE"

"I PAY INTO MY PENSION EVERY MONTH"

What is saving?

Saving is simply putting money away for the future. Some people are much better at it than others! The problem is that you can only spend money once. To save, you have to put off purchases until later. Making plans to save can be upset when the desire to buy something now is overwhelming. Have you ever had that feeling?

All the quotes above show reasons why people save. Some people just save for short periods; others save for long periods. The length of time is important because it helps you to decide where to put your savings. Here are some examples of things you might want to save up for, and how you might do this:

>> Saving for trousers. If you want to save over a few weeks, you might just keep some money at home or leave it in your bank account until you have enough.

>> Saving for a holiday or a car. You have to be much more determined to save over a long period of time. Putting your money into a separate account at the bank can make it a little more difficult to spend. Some bank accounts pay more **interest** if you leave the money in for a longer period of time.

>> Saving to buy a house. Buying a house is the biggest purchase that most of us make. In order to borrow money, we have to show the bank or building society that we are responsible citizens.

By having saved regularly with them and having a steady income, a bank can see that we will be able to repay the money regularly.

>> Saving for a **pension**. Pensions keep us in our retirement. Many of us live for twenty years or more when our working lives are over. It is important to be sure that there is enough money available to make life comfortable as we grow old. The money has to be gathered while we are working in order to be sure that there is enough for later.

Pensions can be provided in different ways:

>> Some businesses pay all the contributions into the pension fund

>> Some organizations share the contributions with the staff

>> Self-employed people have to make their own arrangements

>> The government provides pensions, but they are now small.

Some people chose to pay into a scheme of their own so that they have extra money when they retire.

However a pension is organized, the idea is the same. Money that is saved earns interest and therefore grows larger in the years when we are at work. The money is often put into the hands of organizations that specialize in making it grow.

In an emergency

Things can always go wrong! You might rip your favourite trousers. The car might break down. The central heating might go

People borrow large amounts of money to buy a property.

wrong. All these things are going to cost money to put right. Unless you have some savings, it can be difficult to deal with unexpected events.

> Do you save? When do you save? How do you save? Why do you think it's important to save?

WHERE DO I FIT IN?
Shall I borrow?

"But I must have that!" Karen exploded. She had spotted the perfect top. It would go with everything in her wardrobe.

"But you haven't got any money left," replied Anna.

"Never mind, I've got my **credit card** in my bag" said Karen as she started to rummage for the card.

"But you told me that you hadn't paid off last month's bill in full," added Anna as she tried to persuade her friend from spending.

"Oh stop going on about it. I want the top. It will sort itself out. I'm sure the boss is going to promote me soon and then I can pay it all off."

> Do you think Karen will end up in difficulties? Why?

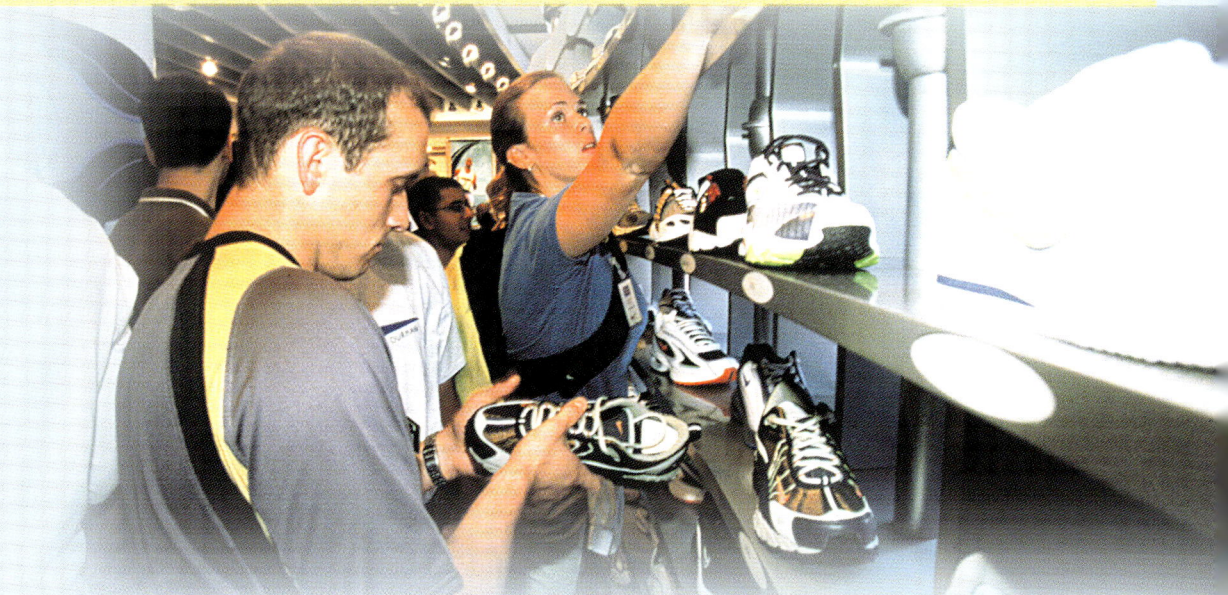

With all the temptations of the consumer society, it is very easy to spend more than you can afford.

Saving and borrowing

When people save money in the bank, it gives the bank the basis for lending to other people. Once again, money is moving around the **economy**.

Borrowing money

To borrow money, you generally need to show that you can repay the debt. A bank wants the security of knowing that it will get its money back. If it thinks that a customer is risky, it will charge a higher **interest rate**. There are several ways of borrowing money – here are some of them.

Ways of borrowing

>> Credit cards. These are the easiest way of borrowing money, but you have to be careful. A bill comes each month to tell you how much you have spent. If you pay it all off, you pay no **interest**. If you don't, you can pay very high rates of interest and your borrowing can be very expensive.

>> **Overdrafts**. Banks give customers permission to 'overdraw' on their bank account when they trust them to repay the money. When people have a pay cheque going into an account regularly, an overdraft can help in a month when there has been an unexpected expense.

>> **Loans.** If you want to buy a a large item such as a car, you may need to borrow money. A loan is made for a fixed amount of time and repayments are planned for each month.

Sometimes people who cannot borrow from anyone else turn to businesses that lend money more flexibly. These often charge very high interest rates, so it is sensible to avoid them.

Businesses borrow

Businesses may borrow money to survive or to grow. In difficult times, a business may not be able to make ends meet, just like individuals. As long as the bank has confidence that the business will recover, it will lend money to help.

A business that wants to expand can turn to the bank to borrow money for new equipment or to help finance a move to a bigger office or factory. The bank will expect the money to be repaid at regular intervals.

Governments borrow, too

The government spends the money that it raises from taxation. Sometimes it needs to spend more. As the sums involved are large, it can't just go to the bank like the rest of us. It issues **bonds** that are sold to organizations, like **pensions** funds (see page 35), which want to make people's money grow in value. The bond has a fixed life span. At the end of its life, it is worth more because it has earned interest.

Sensible borrowing

Businesses, governments and people all borrow money. It can be very helpful at difficult moments. It also allows us to do things immediately that we would otherwise have to save for. Whoever we are, it is important to borrow sensibly. This means thinking carefully about how we can repay the money. If repayment is a problem, it is worth thinking hard about whether the purchase is really necessary.

FIND OUT...

Banks all have leaflets about ways in which you can borrow money. Choose a bank and find out about its range of borrowing facilities.

>> 37

WHERE DO I FIT IN?
Change your money

Countries around the world have different currencies (the type or system of money used). If you travel to Disney World in Florida, USA, you will have to change your pounds to dollars. This is an easy process, as banks everywhere change money. Sometimes you can buy more dollars for your pounds; other times you cannot buy as many. This all depends on what's going on in the countries' **economies**.

Buying foreign currency

When you go off on holiday to a country with a different currency, you need to go to the bank or travel agent to change your money. To decide how much you will receive, the bank will check its list of **exchange rates**. The list shows how many dollars, kröner, yen or any other currency you can buy for one pound.

Exchange rates can also be found every day in the newspapers. There is usually a short list of 'Tourist Rates', which covers most of the places that we go on holiday.

The bank will usually charge a fee, known as **commission**, for changing your money. Some places that change money have signs saying 'No Commission'. Be careful because it probably means that the exchange rate is poor, so you will not get as much of the foreign currency for your pounds.

Why the difference?

Currencies are bought and sold on 'money markets' round the world. These markets trade currencies just like any other product. The trade takes place because governments, businesses and people all want to buy currencies.

There are also organizations that aim to make a **profit** from buying and selling currencies. They are known as **speculators**.

The amount of any currency that dealers on the money market want to buy will depend on how they expect that currency's value to change. If they think that the dollar will be worth more in three months time, they will buy. If they think that it will be worth less, they will sell. If many people buy dollars, the price goes up. In other words, you have to pay more pounds to buy them. If people sell dollars, the price will fall.

The changing value of currency often depends on the state of the economy. If **inflation** is lower in the UK, than in other countries, our products will become cheaper compared to theirs. People overseas will want to buy them, so they will need to buy pounds to do the deal. If lots of people want pounds, the value will go up.

The Euro

A group of countries in the **European Union** has joined together under one currency – the **Euro**. These countries do not have to worry about exchange rates between their countries any more.

Businesses can trade with other countries in the group without having to change money. In the past, the value of the individual country's currencies would go up and down against each other, so it was difficult for businesses to plan ahead. They still have to change their Euros for dollars, yen or any other currency if they want to travel beyond the **Eurozone**.

Not all people agree about the benefits of the Euro. Some fear that the separate countries will find it difficult to control their own economies.

FIND OUT...

Find out more about the Euro by going to the website of the European Union. www.europa.eu.int/euro

FIND OUT...

Choose the currency of a country that you would like to visit. Track it in the newspaper to see how it changes against the pound. Listen to the news and see if you can find out why the currency is changing in value.

A one Euro coin.

WHERE DO I FIT IN?
Who will I vote for?

You have a chance to change the party that governs the country once every four to five years at a General Election. Each area, or constituency, elects a Member of Parliament (MP). The political party that takes power will be the one with the most MPs. If your MP resigns between General Elections, there will be a bi-election in the constituency.

At a local level, you can make a choice every three years. The members of the council in your area are often elected because of their views on a mix of local and national issues.

Whenever you have the opportunity to vote, there are some questions to consider before you make up your mind.

Questions to ask yourself

>> About spending.
Remembering that we can't have everything we want, you need to decide what is important to you. Do you want better health care or education, more roads or defence? In making your decisions, you also need to think about changing things that will improve everyone's way of life, as there will be spin offs for individuals. If, for example, driving cars leads to global warming, is it worth spending money on public transport in order to persuade people to leave their cars at home?

Pairs of tellers count ballot papers in the 2001 General Election. The ballot boxes are on the floor behind them.

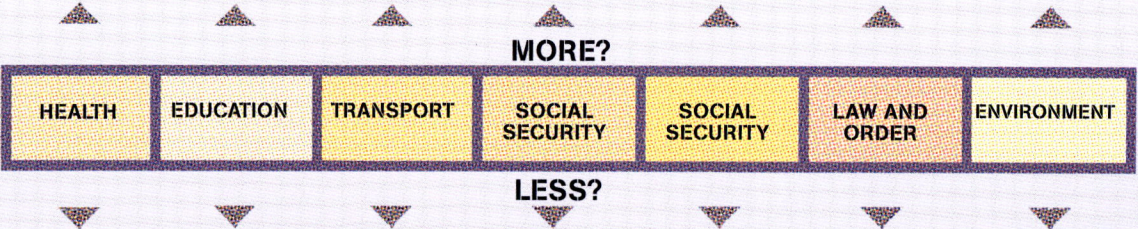

MORE?

HEALTH	EDUCATION	TRANSPORT	SOCIAL SECURITY	SOCIAL SECURITY	LAW AND ORDER	ENVIRONMENT

LESS?

>> About taxation.

When you have made up your mind about what you think is important, you then have to think about where the money comes from. Is it worth paying more **tax** for the things that you think are important? If you do, should it be on **income tax** or VAT? Perhaps **corporation tax** should be increased, but remember that companies paying the tax may put up prices if you do. You have to think about the side effects of you decisions.

FIND OUT... 🔍 >>

When you have worked out what you would like to happen, find out about the views of the political parties and decide which one you would vote for. You can find a list of the website addresses for the political parties on page 5 of this book.

MORE?

INCOME TAX	VALUE ADDED TAX	EXCISE DUTY	CORPORATION TAX

LESS?

Local decisions

Deciding which party to vote for in the local elections is often a mix of considering:

>> what is going on in the local area

>> the views of the political parties.

Some people vote differently in a local election because they feel that one political party deals with local issues better the others.

FIND OUT... 🔍 >>

Are there any local issues being discussed where you live? Perhaps a new road is planned or the town centre is to be pedestrianized. Is there a need for a new sports centre?
What do the local political parties think? How would you vote?

Vote, Vote, Vote!

People often say that there is no point in voting because one vote won't make any difference. The same people are often also heard to complain bitterly about what's going on! The election is the time when you can make your voice heard. Even if the party that you support does not win, the government's actions are often affected by the knowledge that a large part of the **electorate** want something else. Every vote counts.

>> **41**

DEBATE
Issues for discussion

Does inflation matter?

This is an important question that is hard to answer, but governments often put it at the top of their list.

Some issues to think about are:

>> How are individuals affected?

>> How are businesses affected?

>> How does it affect our trade with other countries?

>> How does **inflation** in the UK compare with other countries?

Is unemployment a problem?

The number of people who are unemployed changes over time. Find out how many are unemployed at the moment. Are they male, female, young or old?

Some issues to think about are:

>> What effect does lack of work have on the unemployed?

>> What effect does lack of work have on the **economy**?

>> How does unemployment in the UK compare with other countries?

>> Governments have a range of strategies that they can use to help the unemployed. Find out what is happening now.

FIND OUT... 🔍 >>

What is the rate of inflation at the moment? What do people expect to happen to inflation in the future? Go to www.treasury.gov.uk and look at the latest economic indicators, which will tell you what is happening.

Should people drive cars?

As our environment is threatened by our activities, we need to think carefully about how we treat it. Cars are a vital part of our transport network, but should we be persuading people out of their cars and onto public transport?

People often think that this is an 'environmental' question, but economics is at the heart of it because the answer is all about who pays and who benefits.

Some issues to think about are:

>> Why do we need cars, vans and lorries?

>> What problems do they cause?

>> Who do these problems affect?

>> Who pays the bill for sorting out the problems?

Is there a better way of dealing with the problems? Think carefully about your suggestion. Does it solve the problem? Is it fair?

Should we join the Euro?

Before the UK joins the **Euro**, there will be a **referendum** in which we all have a vote. How would you vote?

Some issues to think about are:

>> How will it help business?

>> How will it affect individuals?

>> What has happened to the countries that are already part of it?

>> What will happen if we don't join?

If there was an election next week…

Who would you vote for and why? Consider the ways in which you want a government to spend our money. Think about how you would raise the money.

>> Has the existing government been successful? Has it met the promises it made before the last election?

>> Is the economy growing? In other words, are we producing more, and are more people employed?

>> Are there any issues that you think are really important that are being ignored?

Take a vote and see which party will win. Make sure that you can explain your own voting decision!

FURTHER RESOURCES

What's happened to unemployment in the UK?

These figures show what happened to the percentage of people unemployed through the 1990s.

1992	9.7
1993	10.3
1994	9.6
1995	8.6
1996	8.2
1997	7.1
1998	6.1
1999	6.0

Source: Annual Abstract of Statistics 2000, ONS

How many people are unemployed in Europe?

These figures show the percentage of people who are unemployed in countries which are members of the European Union.

Belgium	9.2	Luxembourg	2.3
Denmark	5.2	Netherlands	3.3
Greece	10.7	Austria	3.7
Spain	15.9	Portugal	4.5
France	11.3	Finland	10.2
Ireland	5.8	Sweden	7.2
Italy	11.3	UK	6.1

Sources: European Statistical Pocket Book 2000, European Communities

>>

What's happening to prices?

These figures show how much consumer prices went up as a percentage.

Belgium	0.6	Luxembourg	1.0
Denmark	1.6	Netherlands	2.2
Greece	2.5	Austria	0.6
Spain	2.3	Portugal	2.3
France	0.5	Finland	1.2
Ireland	1.6	Sweden	0.5
Italy	1.7	UK	1.6

Source: World Economic and Social Survey 2000, UN

Where do our imports come from?

These figures show the main countries which sell things to the UK in 000 millions.

European Union	£102.8
USA	£25.7
Japan	£9.5
Switzerland	£5
Hong Kong	£4.6
Norway	£3.6
China	£3
Singapore	£2.5

Source: Annual Abstract of Statistics 2000, ONS

Where do our exports go?

These figures show the main countries which buy things from the UK in 000 millions.

European Union	£95.6
USA	£22
Japan	£3.2
Switzerland	£3
Norway	£2.8
Hong Kong	£2.7
Saudi Arabia	£2.7
Australia	£2.3

Source: Annual Abstract of Statistics 2000, ONS

Useful websites

The HM Treasury website tells you about issues such as the budget and the government's financial policies:
www.hm-treasury.gov.uk

The *Financial Times* website tells you about financial news from across the world:
http://news.ft.com/home/uk

The Bank of England has a website, which tells you about its function, history and give links to relevant websites:
www.bankofengland.co.uk

GLOSSARY

added value — the difference between the cost of the resources used in making a product and the price that people are prepared to pay

Bank of England — the bank that prints bank notes, sets interest rates and looks after the UK's financial system

benefits — payments made by the government to help people meet basic needs

bonds — certificates which can be bought from the government or an organization, which promise to repay the money lent to it at a set rate of interest

Budget — this happens every year. It is when the Chancellor of the Exchequer, who runs the country's finances, explains how the government will raise and spend its money.

business rates — these are rates paid by all the businesses in an area. The amount a business pays depends on the rent that could be charged for their premises.

commission — banks and travel agents charge this for changing money from one currency to another

corporation tax — a tax paid to the government by companies on their profits

costs — the amount of money that a business spends on the resources needed to make its products

council tax — a tax paid by everyone who lives in a certain area. It is based on the value of the taxpayer's house.

credit cards — these are used to buy things. A bill is sent to the customer once a month. If it is paid immediately, no interest is paid. If no payment is made or the bill is not settled in full, interest is added to the account.

discrimination — making an unfair judgment about people based upon their differences, for example colour, culture or disability

economy — the economy includes everyone who spends and earns money. People, businesses and the government are all part of it.

electorate — the group of people in a country who are allowed to vote

Euro — the new currency of the European Union, which replaces the currencies of twelve member states

Eurozone — the group of European Union countries that use the Euro as currency.

European Union — a group of fifteen member states that trade freely and allow people to move from country to country with no controls. The countries work together politically also.

exchange rate — this gives the value of one currency in terms of another

exports — services and goods that are sold to other countries

imports — services and goods that are bought from other countries

income tax — the tax that must be paid to the government on personal income

inflation — a continuing rise in prices. This means that money will not buy as much.

interest — the cost charged for of borrowing money or paid out to savers

interest rates	the annual cost of a loan. A 10% interest rate means that 10% must be paid each year as a cost of borrowing the money – so if you borrowed £100, and repaid the loan over a year, you would pay back a total of £110.
loans	these are made by a bank for a fixed amount of money and over a fixed period of time. They will be repaid at regular intervals.
manifesto	a political party's statement of what it plans to do and how it plans to raise the money it needs to carry it out
manufacturing	producing a physical product including, all sorts of things we buy, from computers to trainers
Monetary Policy Committee	a group of economic experts that sets the rate of interest every month
multinational	a business that has interests in several countries
National Insurance	a system where employed people pay money to the government to pay for social services, state assistance for the sick or unemployed and pensions for the retired
overdrafts	these allow people to borrow just the amount of money they need. The bank will set a limit on the amount that an account can be 'overdrawn'.
pensions	money paid to people when they retire from work. They may come from the government, the employer or the individual who has saved during their working life.
profit	the difference between costs and revenue
progressive tax	a tax that rises as people earn more
referendum	a vote on one issue
regressive tax	a tax that is a higher proportion of income for those on lower pay
resources	things needed to make a product or provide a service, such as equipment, buildings, people and materials
revenue	the amount of money a business receives from selling its product, or money raised by the government
service	something provided by people for other people. Hairdressers, estate agents and dentists all provide a service.
shareholders	people who have bought and own shares in a company
Stock Exchange	the market in which stacks and shares are bought and sold
social services	services provided by the government or state for the community, including education and medical care
speculators	people who buy and sell currencies to make a profit
stakeholders	the groups of people who are affected by a business's activities
tax	money paid to the government by people and businesses based on their spending and earning. It is used to pay for everything that the government provides.
transaction	an exchange of money for a product or a service
unemployment figures	produced by the government, these figures include everyone who is seeking work and claiming benefit

INDEX

Titles in the *Citizen's Guide* series include:

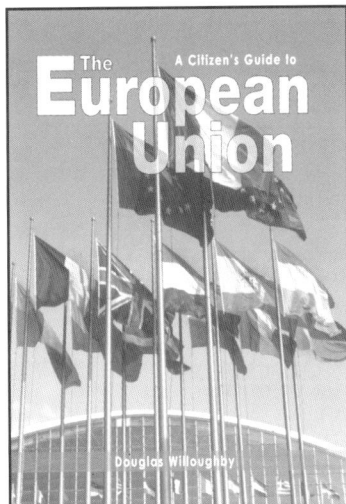

Hardback   0 431 14493 1

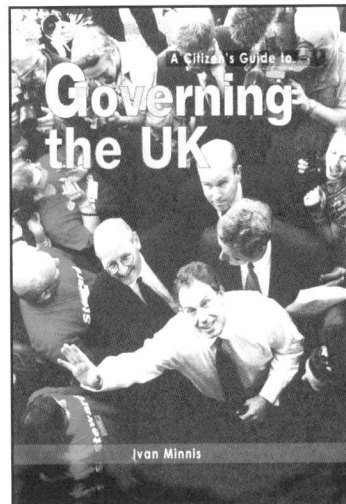

Hardback   0 431 14492 3

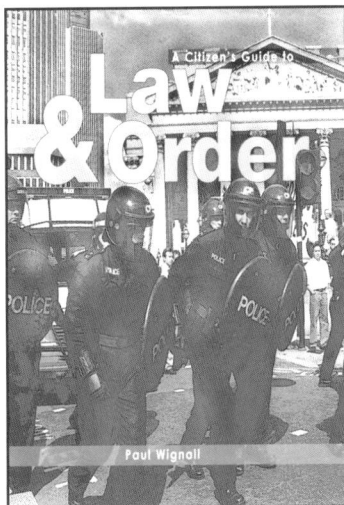

Hardback   0 431 14495 8

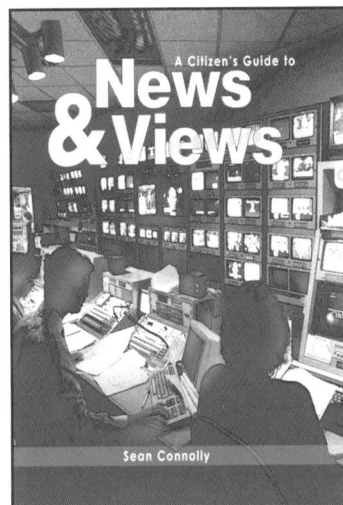

Hardback   0 431 14491 5

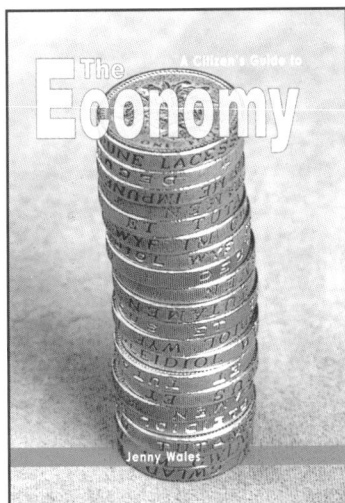

Hardback   0 431 14494 X

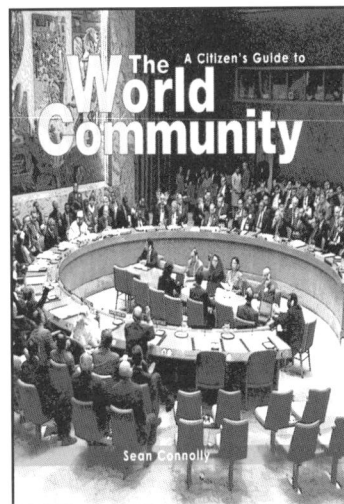

Hardback   0 431 14490 7

Find out about the other titles in this series on our website www.heinemann.co.uk/library